OCT 2007

Arctic Ocean

30°E 60° 90° 120° 150°

EUROPE

A

S

I

A

CHINA

A

AFRICA

Pacific

Ocean

Indian

Ocean

AUSTRALIA

ANTARCTICA

Countries of the World

China

Jen Green

George Wei and Hanchao Lu, Consultants

NATIONAL GEOGRAPHIC

WASHINGTON, D.C.

Contents

Foreword

China is a land of contrasts and surprises: China is about the same size as the United States, but it has five times the population; China has only about 7 percent of the world's farmland, but it feeds 22 percent of all the people on Earth; China is the home of one of the world's oldest civilizations, but it has only recently become a "modern" nation.

Of all the world's early civilizations, the Chinese civilization stands out for its vitality and continuity. Chinese writing can be traced back to the 1700s B.C. when inscriptions scratched on ox bones were used to predict the future. China became a vast, politically unified state in 221 B.C. at a time when Europe was still divided into small, squabbling states. And for at least 2,000 years, the teachings of a philosopher called Confucius have been at the core of the Chinese way of life. He taught that human beings can learn, improve, and move toward perfection through their personal actions and their involvement in the community.

This vast and old civilization has been confronted with tremendous challenges in the last 150 years. When Western powers became involved in China in the mid-19th century, their actions helped bring about wars, revolutions, reforms, and horrendous suffering as the Chinese people adjusted to the changes in their society.

Since the early 1980s, China has been undergoing what many Western observers call a "quiet revolution" in which the country's economy has been transformed from one that is controlled centrally by the government to one that allows individual enterprise. As a result China is rapidly becoming a dominant force in the world's economy. At the same time, all aspects of Chinese life are changing dramatically.

This book introduces this ancient and fascinating country, covering topics such as land and people, ecology and environment, history and philosophy, culture and customs, technology and inventions, politics and the economy. Many experts predict that the 21st century will be the "Chinese century." Whether or not that proves to be true, there is no doubt that what happens in China will likely affect many other nations around the world.

▲ This lone cyclist is dwarfed by the expressways and high-rise buildings of modern Beijing (Peking).

Hanchao Lu

Hanchao Lu, Ph.D.
Professor of History and Director of Graduate Studies
School of History, Technology, & Society
Georgia Institute of Technology

A Vast Land

EVEN CHINESE WHO who live on the other side of the country know about the beauty of Guilin. The slow, clear waters of the Li River reflect green hills, towering limestone cliffs, and waterfalls. Poets have celebrated this corner of Guangxi (g-wong-she) province in southern China for centuries. The Chinese call Guilin "Paradise on Earth."

For the fishers of Guilin, life has changed little for centuries. Their bamboo rafts dot the river, and they still use diving birds called cormorants to catch fish. Elsewhere, however, the story is very different. In the last 20 years, China has changed faster than any other country in the world. Cranes tower above construction sites in the growing cities, where booming industries attract millions of people in search of jobs.

◀ There have always been bamboo fishing rafts on the Li River—but these have seats, roofs, and sunshades for the comfort of tourists visiting Guilin.

VARIED CLIMATE

Stretching 3,100 miles (5,000 km) from east to west and 3,400 miles (5,500 km) from north to south, China has a widely varied climate. The far north is icy and subarctic, while the southeast is tropical. Lying between the Asian landmass and the Pacific Ocean, many parts of China are affected by monsoon winds, which change direction regularly twice a year. In winter, cold, dry winds bring dust storms to the north. In summer, moist winds bring rain to the south and east. The map opposite shows the physical features of China. Labels on this map and on similar maps throughout this book identify places pictured in each chapter.

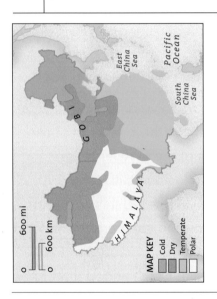

MAP KEY
- Cold
- Dry
- Temperate
- Polar

East China Sea

Pacific Ocean

South China Sea

GOBI

HIMALAYA

600 mi
600 km

Average Temperature & Rainfall

Average High/Low Temperatures; Yearly Rainfall

Harbin, Heilongjiang:
82° F (28° C) / -13° F (-25° C); 22 in (55 cm)

Beijing:
88° F (31° C) / 14° F (-9° C); 25 in (63 cm)

Shanghai:
90° F (32° C) / 32° F (0° C); 45 in (114 cm)

Guangzhou, Guangdong:
91° F (33° C) / 49° F (10° C); 66 in (167 cm)

Xi'an, Shaanxi:
91° F (33° C) / 23° F (-5° C); 23 in (58 cm)

Lhasa, Xizang:
74° F (23° C) / 15° F (-10° C); 17 in (43 cm)

Fast Facts

> **OFFICIAL NAME:** People's Republic of China
> **FORM OF GOVERNMENT:** Communist state
> **CAPITAL:** Beijing (Peking)
> **POPULATION:** 1,306,313,812
> **OFFICIAL LANGUAGE:** Standard Chinese or Mandarin
> **MONETARY UNIT:** yuan (also called renminbi)
> **AREA:** 3,705,405 square miles (9,596,960 square kilometers)
> **BORDERING NATIONS:** Afghanistan, Bhutan, India, Kazakhstan, Kyrgyzstan, Laos, Mongolia, Myanmar, Nepal, North Korea, Pakistan, Russia, Tajikistan, Vietnam
> **HIGHEST POINT:** Mount Everest 29,035 feet (8,850 meters)
> **LOWEST POINT:** Turpan Pendi (Tulufan depression) 505 feet (154 meters) below sea level
> **MAJOR MOUNTAIN RANGES:** Himalaya, Kunlun Shan, Plateau of Tibet, Guizhou-Yunnan Highlands, Qin Ling, and the mountains of Sichuan and Hubei
> **MAJOR RIVERS:** Yangtze (Chang Jiang), Yellow (Huang), Huai, Xi

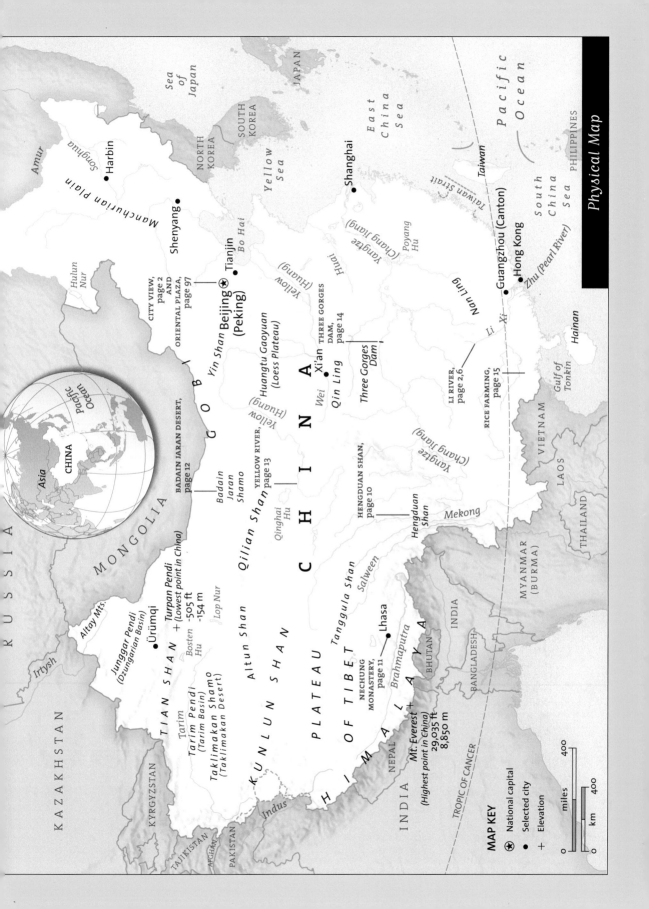

Physical Map

RUSSIA

KAZAKHSTAN

KYRGYZSTAN

TAJIKISTAN

AFGHAN.

PAKISTAN

MONGOLIA

Irtysh

Altay Mts.

Amur

Songhua

Harbin

Manchurian Plain

Hulun Nur

Shenyang

NORTH KOREA

SOUTH KOREA

JAPAN

Sea of Japan

TIAN SHAN

Junggar Pendi (Dzungarian Basin)

Ürümqi

Turpan Pendi
-505 ft (Lowest point in China)
-154 m

Bosten Hu

Lop Nur

Tarim

Tarim Pendi (Tarim Basin)

Taklimakan Shamo (Taklimakan Desert)

Altun Shan

GOBI

BADAIN JARAN DESERT, page 12

Badain Jaran Shamo

Qilian Shan

Yin Shan

YELLOW RIVER, page 13

Qinghai Hu

Yellow (Huang)

Beijing (Peking)

CITY VIEW, page 2 AND ORIENTAL PLAZA, page 97

Tianjin

Bo Hai

Yellow Sea

Huangtu Gaoyuan (Loess Plateau)

C H I N A

Xi'an

Wei

Qin Ling

THREE GORGES DAM, page 14

Three Gorges Dam

Shanghai

East China Sea

Yangtze (Chang Jiang)

Poyang Hu

Huai

KUNLUN SHAN

Tanggula Shan

PLATEAU OF TIBET

Lhasa

NECHUNG MONASTERY, page 11

H I M A L A Y A

Mt. Everest
29,035 ft (Highest point in China)
8,850 m

Brahmaputra

BHUTAN

BANGLADESH

INDIA

NEPAL

Indus

Salween

Mekong

HENGDUAN SHAN, page 10

Hengduan Shan

Yangtze (Chang Jiang)

MYANMAR (BURMA)

LAOS

THAILAND

VIETNAM

Nan Ling

Xi

Li

LI RIVER, page 2,6

RICE FARMING, page 15

Guangzhou (Canton)

Hong Kong

Zhu (Pearl River)

Gulf of Tonkin

Hainan

South China Sea

PHILIPPINES

Taiwan

Taiwan Strait

Pacific Ocean

TROPIC OF CANCER

Asia

CHINA

Pacific Ocean

MAP KEY

⭐ National capital

● Selected city

+ Elevation

miles   0   400

km   0   400

Varied Landscapes

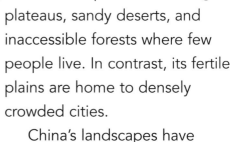

▼ The Hengduan Shan mountains in southwestern China are home to a remarkable variety of animals and plants, like these lady's slipper orchids.

One-fifth of all the people on Earth live in the People's Republic of China. It has the largest population in the world, estimated at 1.3 billion in 2005. Yet China is only the world's fourth largest country. Its 3.7 billion square miles (nearly 9.6 billion sq. km) include high plateaus, sandy deserts, and inaccessible forests where few people live. In contrast, its fertile plains are home to densely crowded cities.

China's landscapes have shaped its history. The deserts protected it from invasion, and the river valleys provided food and shelter for the growing population. The Chinese call their land Zhongguo (chung-gour), meaning the Middle Kingdom. In ancient times they believed that it lay at the center of the world.

The easiest way to get around China is by train. Flying is too expensive for most Chinese, and in many areas, poor roads make it difficult to travel by car. Most people in both the cities and countryside get from place to place by bicycle—or by walking. Like much else, however, this is changing as China builds new roads and airports.

Mountains and Plateaus

China is a land of many mountains. A third of its area is mountainous. The highest mountain on Earth lies on the border between China and Nepal. The Chinese call it Qomolangma; we call it Mount Everest. Like many of its neighboring peaks in the Himalayan range, Mount Everest is always covered with ice and snow. At the top of Everest, the air is so thin that mountaineers have to carry tanks of extra oxygen. North of the Himalaya is the Plateau of Tibet, which is often called the "roof of the world." People who live there get used to breathing the thin air.

▲ Buddhist monks in Tibet perform a sacred ritual against the backdrop of the Himalaya. Buddhist pilgrims from ancient India gave the mountain range its name—"hima" is Sanskrit for "snow," and "alaya" means "abode" or "home."

Desert Mysteries

The desert region north of the Plateau of Tibet is swept by icy winds in winter and baked by the sun in summer. Temperatures in the Turpan Pendi depression can reach 118° F (48° C). The Taklimakan Shamo is Asia's driest desert. It is also the setting for one of China's great mysteries. Buried in the desert sands are mummies over 2,000 years old. They were not wrapped, like Egyptian mummies, but they have been almost perfectly preserved by the dry conditions and the salt in the sandy earth. Archaeologists puzzle over the mummies' fair hair, European facial features, and silk clothing. They think the mummies may have been part of a long-forgotten people.

The Gobi Desert to the east has its own secrets. In the 1920s scientists found a dinosaur skeleton on top of a nest full of eggs. They guessed that the dinosaur had died while stealing the eggs to eat. But 70 years later, scientists found more skeletons and eggs and realized that the dinosaur was a caring parent.

▼ Bactrian camels cross the sand dunes of the Badain Jaran desert. Camels store fat in their humps, so they can survive in places where there is not much to eat. They get most of their water from their food.

Mighty Rivers

China has thousands of rivers. The two most important are the Yangtze (Chang Jiang) and Yellow (Huang) rivers. They both flow through narrow gorges in their upper courses and form swampy deltas where they reach the sea. China's earliest villages sprang up along the banks of the Yellow River and its tributary, the Wei. Throughout history, the Yellow River has watered the surrounding land and made it fertile, but it has also brought terrible floods. It is often known as "China's Sorrow." At 3,915 miles (6,300 km) long, the Yangtze is the world's third longest river. It forms a dividing line between northern and southern China.

▲ The Yellow, or Huang, River is named for the yellow soil that it picks up while making a huge loop through a region called Huangtu Gaoyuan (Yellow or Loess Plateau).

Rice Paddies of the East

China's largest lowlands lie in the east of the country, around the plains of the Yangtze and Yellow rivers and the delta of the Pearl (Zhu) River in the south. A maze of streams and canals irrigate thousands of small paddy fields where farmers grow rice. The fields have to be drained so that the rice can be harvested by hand. Most farm machinery would sink in the muddy

THE THREE GORGES DAM

A s the Yangtze (Chang Jiang) leaves the mountains, it flows through a region of spectacular canyons called the Three Gorges. The Chinese are building the largest dam in the world there to generate electricity from the fast-flowing water. The dam will also help prevent flooding and save water for farming. When it is completed in 2009, the dam will create a reservoir nearly 400 miles (650 km) long and will provide about a tenth of China's energy. However, the creation of the lake has forced some 1.2 million people to move in order to avoid the rising waters. Wildlife experts fear the dam will cause problems for water life downstream.

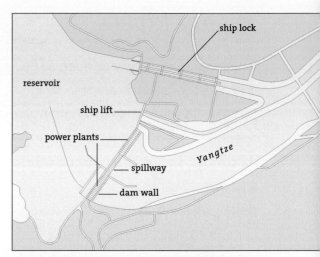

▲ The dam's system of discharge and diversion channels will control flooding. Locks that control the water levels will enable large ships to sail upstream as far as Chongqing.

▼ The Three Gorges Dam is China's biggest engineering project since the Great Wall was built more than 2,000 years ago.

fields. Chinese farmers grow three rice crops a year. The Chinese eat more rice than anything else, so they need a lot! A favorite dish is *zongzi*, dumplings made from sticky rice, often with a filling of mashed yellow beans, meat, or chestnuts.

Expanding Cities

The lowlands of the south and east are the most densely populated areas of China. In all, China has 34 cities with more than a million people. The capital, Beijing (Peking), was the home of the emperors who ruled China from the 15th century until 1912. The port of Shanghai on the Pacific coast is China's largest city and one of the fastest-growing cities in the world. Construction sites in China's cities use so much steel that it has become more expensive all around the world. To avoid traffic jams and pollution in the crowded new cities, the government is looking to the past and telling people to bicycle to work or school.

▲ A farmer uses a water buffalo to plow a rice paddy. The bundles of rice seedlings will be planted by hand.

▼ Oriental Plaza is a new office and hotel development in Beijing.

Natural Marvels

HIGH ON A ROCKY CRAG in frozen Tibet, a snow leopard charges toward its prey. Thanks to the rugged terrain and the cat's shy habits, few people have ever seen a snow leopard. It is well camouflaged by its spotted coat amid the snow and rocks. Yet even in these remote mountains, the big cat is at risk. Hunters kill snow leopards for their beautiful fur. The leopard's bones are also used in traditional Chinese medicine instead of tiger bones. The snow leopard is one of the rarest mammals in the world. Experts believe that only about 2,000 are left in China. The Chinese government has set up reserves to protect the snow leopard. The cat's inaccessible habitat makes it difficult to enforce antihunting laws—but it makes it difficult for the hunters, too.

◀ **The snow leopard mainly hunts wild sheep and goats. It creeps up on its victim, hidden by its camouflage, until it gets close enough to pounce.**

A WEALTH OF WILDLIFE

China has many different habitats, including windswept grasslands, snowy peaks, barren deserts, pine forests, and lush tropical rain forests. Its rivers, lakes, and coastal waters are home to over 3,800 species of fish, several hundred amphibians, and as many reptiles, including the unique Chinese alligator of the eastern marshlands. The map opposite shows the main vegetation zones—what grows where—in China. Each zone is home to a particular set of plants and animals. Unique creatures found wild only in China include the giant panda, golden-haired monkey, Yangtze river dolphin, South China tiger, and brown-eared pheasant.

▲ **The baiji or Yangtze river dolphin hunts fish in the murky water by sending out a stream of clicking sounds and listening for the echoes that bounce back off its prey.**

Species at Risk

The wildlife of China's forests is threatened by logging for timber and clear-cutting for farming. Deserts are expanding as the surrounding grasslands are nibbled bare by sheep and cattle. However, the Chinese government is aware of the importance of its wild areas and the animals that live in them. China has over 1,270 reserves, covering 12 percent of its total area, and more reserves are planned to protect 16 percent of China by 2010.

Species at risk include:

> Giant panda
> Pere David's deer
> Golden-haired monkey
> Yangtze alligator
> Yangtze river dolphin
> Snow leopard
> Wild yak
> Red-crowned crane
> South China tiger
> Manchurian tiger
> Indo-Chinese tiger
> Crested ibis
> Asian elephant
> Brown eared pheasant

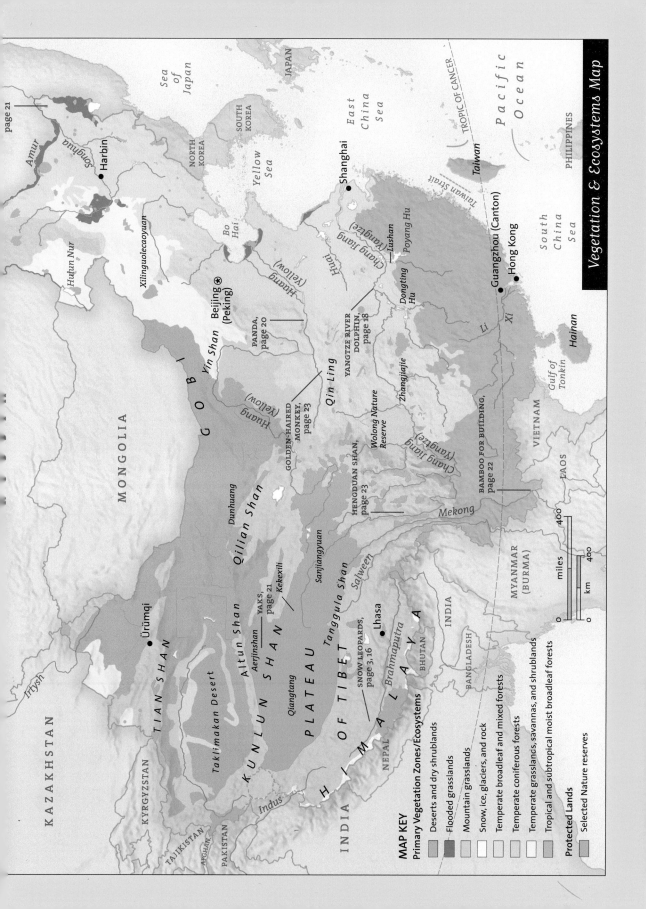

Vegetation & Ecosystems Map

MAP KEY

Primary Vegetation Zones/Ecosystems

- Deserts and dry shrublands
- Flooded grasslands
- Mountain grasslands
- Snow, ice, glaciers, and rock
- Temperate broadleaf and mixed forests
- Temperate coniferous forests
- Temperate grasslands, savannas, and shrublands
- Tropical and subtropical moist broadleaf forests

Protected Lands

- Selected Nature reserves

KAZAKHSTAN

KYRGYZSTAN

TAJIKISTAN

AFGHAN.

PAKISTAN

Irtysh

TIAN SHAN

Ürümqi

Taklimakan Desert

KUNLUN SHAN

Altun Shan

Qiangtang

Aerjinshan

YAKS,
page 21

Kekexili

Qilian Shan

Dunhuang

Sanjiangyuan

PLATEAU

Tanggula Shan

OF TIBET

SNOW LEOPARDS,
page 3, 16

Lhasa

Salween

Indus

Brahmaputra

NEPAL

BHUTAN

H   I   M   A   L   A   Y   A

INDIA

BANGLADESH

INDIA

Mekong

MYANMAR
(BURMA)

HENGDUAN SHAN,
page 23

Wolong Nature
Reserve

Zhangjiajie

Chang Jiang
(Yangtze)

BAMBOO FOR BUILDING,
page 22

LAOS

VIETNAM

Gulf of
Tonkin

Li

Xi

Hainan

GOLDEN-HAIRED
MONKEY, page 23

Huang
(Yellow)

Qin Ling

YANGTZE RIVER
DOLPHIN,
page 18

Dongting
Hu

Hong Kong

Guangzhou (Canton)

South
China
Sea

PHILIPPINES

MONGOLIA

G   O   B   I

Yin Shan

Beijing
(Peking) ✴

PANDA,
page 20

Huang
(Yellow)

Huai

Chang Jiang (Yangtze)

Poyang Hu

Lushan

Shanghai

East
China
Sea

Bo
Hai

Yellow
Sea

NORTH
KOREA

SOUTH
KOREA

JAPAN

Sea
of
Japan

Xilinguolecaoyuan

Hulun Nur

Harbin

Amur

Songhua

page 21

Taiwan

Taiwan Strait

TROPIC OF CANCER

Pacific
Ocean

miles

km

0   400

0   400

THE GIANT PANDA

The misty mountains of southwest China are home to the giant panda, a mammal that lives nowhere else. This bear needs to live near stands of bamboo, whose leaves and stems provide its only food. The panda plucks bamboo by using a bony knob on its wrist, which acts as an extra thumb. Bamboo contains little nourishment, so pandas have to eat huge amounts: They spend up to 16 hours a day eating. That's longer than many people are awake. In the past, pandas were hunted for their fur and also for use in Chinese medicine. About 1,600 are left. They live mainly in reserves, guarded by wardens. The panda is an international symbol of the conservation movement—the effort to protect rare animals and plants.

▲ The panda is one of the official mascots of the 2008 Olympic Games in Beijing (Peking).

Tough Survivors

Only about a tenth of China is suitable for farming. The rest is too cold, high, dry, or stony for tender crops to grow. That leaves plenty of space for wildlife, but plants and animals have had to adapt to the harsh conditions. And everywhere in China, they sometimes come into conflict with humans.

The snowy plateau of Tibet is home to yaks—bulky cattle with long, shaggy fur, which keeps them warm even in howling blizzards. Yaks are vital for the people that can survive the cold, and so stay on the trees year-round. The forests are home to the elk, caribou, bear, and musk deer. Male musk deer are hunted for the smelly substance produced by their scent glands called musk. It is used to make perfumes and traditional East Asian medicines. Other forest residents include the Siberian (Manchurian) tiger. It is the largest tiger in the world and also the rarest. Experts believe that only a few hundred of these striped hunters are left.

Rain Forest Life

Tropical rain forests contain more plants and animals than any other kind of habitat, and the forests of southern China are no exception. In the far south, Yunnan province is known as the "kingdom of flowers" because it has more than 2,500 different plant varieties, while Wolong Nature Reserve in neighboring Sichuan holds 4,000 types of plants. Xishuangbanna Reserve (she-shuang-ban-na) in the far south has tigers, elephants, monkeys, and gibbons—shaggy-haired apes that use their long arms to swing through the trees. Birds called hornbills build an unusual nest: The male uses mud to seal the female inside a hollow tree while she sits on her eggs and then he feeds her through a slit in the mud.

▲ Rhododendrons bloom in the Xiao Nong Valley of Yunnan. Behind are the peaks of the Hengduan Shan.

▼ The golden-haired monkey gives birth to only one baby at a time.

A Rich and Ancient Past

N 1974 FARMERS digging a well in northwest China found the head of a terra-cotta soldier. When archaeologists investigated, they dug up warrior after warrior. The life-size statues formed a formidable underground army of about 7,000 foot soldiers, archers, and charioteers that stood guard over a nearby artificial hill. The hill enclosed the tomb of a Chinese emperor known as Qin Shi Huangdi, the First Emperor of the Qin dynasty.

Qin Shi Huangdi was a mighty warrior who united China in 221 B.C. China remained a great empire until the 19th century, when the emperors' control grew weak. The last emperor was overthrown in 1912, and China became a republic. In 1949, after a bitter civil war, it became a communist country.

◀ No two members of the terra-cotta army are the same. Every facial expression and hairstyle is different, and the soldiers carry a range of weapons.

THE DYNASTIES

C hinese history is divided into dynasties, each of which marks the period when a line of emperors ruled. These dynasties were often periods of relative peace and prosperity, during which art, science, and literature flourished. In between were troubled times, when China was torn by wars.

China became an empire in 221 B.C. under Qin Shi Huangdi, who founded the Qin dynasty. Later rulers expanded China's territory. The extent of the empire during the Qin and Tang dynasties is shown on the map opposite. Each new dynasty tended to found

a new capital as its power base. China's many former capitals include Xianyang under the Qin and Chang'an (modern Xi'an) under the Han.

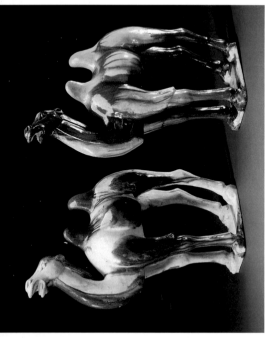

▼ Tang potters were very creative, inventing a number of new techniques. Many of the pieces they made, like these Bactrian camels, were buried with important people for use in the afterlife.

Time line

This chart shows the approximate dates for major dynasties that ruled China between 206 B.C. and A.D. 1912.

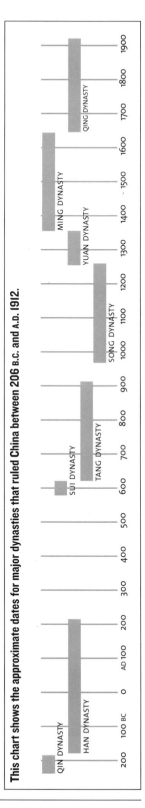

QIN DYNASTY

HAN DYNASTY

SUI DYNASTY

TANG DYNASTY

SONG DYNASTY

YUAN DYNASTY

MING DYNASTY

QING DYNASTY

200 BC 100 BC 0 AD 100 200 300 400 500 600 700 800 900 1000 1100 1200 1300 1400 1500 1600 1700 1800 1900

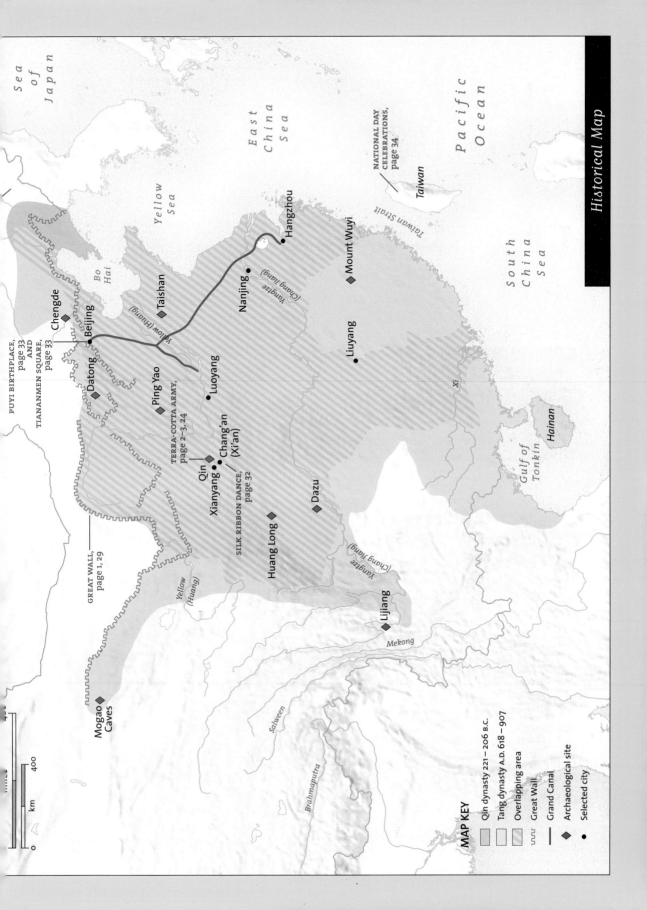

Historical Map

Sea of Japan

East China Sea

Pacific Ocean

Yellow Sea

South China Sea

Taiwan Strait

Taiwan

NATIONAL DAY CELEBRATIONS, page 34

Hangzhou

Mount Wuyi

Nanjing

Yangtze (Chang Jiang)

Bo Hai

Taishan

Liuyang

Chengde

Beijing

Xi

Hainan

Yellow (Huang)

Luoyang

Gulf of Tonkin

PUYI BIRTHPLACE, page 33 AND TIANANMEN SQUARE, page 33

Datong

Ping Yao

TERRA-COTTA ARMY, page 2–3, 24

Chang'an (Xi'an)

Qin

Xianyang

SILK RIBBON DANCE, page 32

Dazu

Huang Long

GREAT WALL, page 1, 29

Yellow (Huang)

Yangtze (Chang Jiang)

Lijiang

Mogao Caves

Mekong

Salween

Brahmaputra

km

400

0

400

MAP KEY

- Qin dynasty 221–206 B.C.
- Tang dynasty A.D. 618–907
- Overlapping area
- Great Wall
- Grand Canal
- ◆ Archaeological site
- • Selected city

The Beginnings of Civilization

The Chinese are proud of their long history. About 5,000 years ago the first settlements grew up along the banks of the Yellow (Huang) River. The people built walls around their villages to keep out attackers and grew wheat, millet, vegetables, and fruit. About 4,000 years ago, they learned how to make pottery and invented a system of writing. They also learned to make bronze and iron for tools and weapons. Gradually, their villages grew into towns.

THE EMPEROR'S WALL

Ying Zheng, prince of Qin in northwest China, defeated his rivals and proclaimed himself the first emperor of Qin: Qin Shi Huangdi. The word China is thought to come from the name Qin, which is pronounced "Chin." Ying Zheng set up a strong government and introduced standard weights and measures, language, and currency throughout his empire. He also began to build a vast wall along China's northern boundary, to guard against invasion by Mongol tribes. The wall had watchtowers and heavily guarded gates. The top was wide enough for horsemen to ride along to face the enemy or to carry messages. Over the centuries, later emperors made the wall stronger and longer. Eventually, the wall stretched for about 4,500 miles (7,300 km), making it the largest artificial structure on Earth. The Great Wall now draws tourists from all over the world. It can even be seen from space.

Dynastic Rule

China's first kings ruled only a small part of the modern country. But in 221 B.C., a prince named Ying Zheng united several kingdoms to become China's first emperor. Like all later emperors, he changed his name when he came to power: Ying became Qin Shi Huangdi. Later emperors built on his achievements, and China grew larger and more powerful. Each dynasty, or family of rulers, achieved

new things. The Han emperors developed China's administration. The Sui and Tang dynasties were golden ages of art and architecture. The Song were great canal-builders. The Ming period is famous for its beautiful white-and-blue porcelain.

Invented in China

Ancient China was a land of invention. For centuries, China was way ahead of most other countries

▲ The Great Wall was built by forced labor; many workers died from the hard conditions.

▼ The Han were skilled at casting bronze, like this scene of a wild animal attacking a bird.

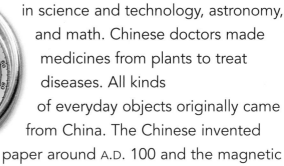

▶ The Chinese developed the compass so they could build houses facing north, which they thought brought good fortune.

▼ China is still the world's biggest producer of one of their most famous inventions: fireworks.

in science and technology, astronomy, and math. Chinese doctors made medicines from plants to treat diseases. All kinds of everyday objects originally came from China. The Chinese invented paper around A.D. 100 and the magnetic compass about a hundred years later. They used their compasses to tell fortunes and locate lucky sites for buildings long before they used them for finding their way. The Chinese had invented printing by 500—nearly a thousand years before it was invented anywhere else. Porcelain, silk, stirrups for horse-riding, and the crossbow were all in daily use in China centuries before they reached the West. The first Europeans to visit China were particularly impressed by two inventions: gunpowder and fireworks.

Town Planning

The Chinese were skilled architects and builders. As the capital of the Tang dynasty from the seventh to the tenth centuries, the city of Chang'an became a model for cities all over Asia. Other cities were jumbled and chaotic: Chang'an was laid out in a neat grid. There were separate districts for the emperor and his servants, noble families, merchants, craftsmen, and the poor.

Like the cities, Chinese society also had a well-defined structure, with four classes below the emperor. At the top were nobles, landowners, and scholars. Then came farmers, who are traditionally respected in China, followed by craftsmen. At the bottom of the pile were merchants. They were seen as lowly, even though some of them became very rich.

The Last Dynasty

From 1279 to 1368 China was ruled by Mongol emperors. Then came the Ming dynasty and finally the Qing. The Qing rulers came from Manchuria, in northern China.

At first the Qing ruled well, but gradually they grew weaker. During the 1800s, a series of terrible

KUBLAI KHAN AND MONGOL RULE

In the 1200s China was threatened by warlike Mongols, skilled horsemen from the grasslands to the north. In 1215 the Mongol leader Genghis Khan swept south to capture Beijing (Peking). In 1279 Genghis's grandson, Kublai Khan, conquered all of China. China became part of the Mongol Empire, which covered all of Central Asia. Kublai's dynasty, the Yuan, ruled China for nearly a century.

The Mongols brought peace and prosperity. The emperors were eager to trade with other countries, and travelers began to visit China. In 1275 Marco Polo, an Italian merchant from Venice, became one of the first Europeans to see the court of Kublai Khan. Polo spent 17 years in China, and his book on Chinese culture became a best-seller in Europe. The Venetian helped introduce many aspects of Chinese culture to the West.

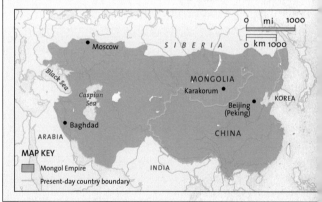

THE SILK ROAD

From about 200 B.C. to A.D. 1500, trade routes linked China to Europe and the Mediterranean. The 4,000-mile (6,500-km) network is known as the Silk Road because of its most precious cargo. Silk was made in China from 3000 B.C., but Europeans only learned how to make it in the sixth century A.D., after monks smuggled two silkworms out of China in hollow walking sticks. Few people traveled the whole route. They sold their goods to other merchants. Caravans of camels and mules carried silk, porcelain, and jade to Europe, while gold, silver, wool, and linen passed the other way.

▲ This silk ribbon dance was inspired by the prosperous cities of the Silk Road.

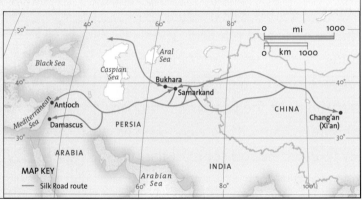

floods and earthquakes brought great hardship to China. Many poor Chinese blamed the emperors from Manchuria for their troubles.

The Qing resisted change and tried to prevent trade or other contact with the West. European nations gradually overtook China in industry and technology. As the Qing grew weaker, British traders forced the Chinese to sell them silk, tea, and porcelain, which were highly popular in Britain. In return, the British sold the Chinese a drug called opium, which was grown in India. Many Chinese became addicted to the drug, which made it difficult for them to do any work. When the Qing tried to ban the trade in opium, the British fought and won two wars against China. The British forced the Chinese to give

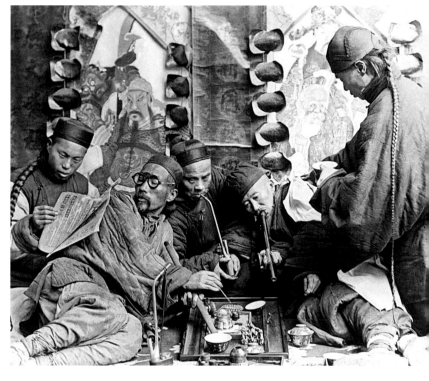

them trading rights and territory, including the island of Hong Kong. Countries such as France, Germany, and Japan also gained territory and influence in China.

Groups opposed to the Qing formed throughout China. In 1911 they rose up in rebellion. The last Chinese emperor, Puyi, was forced to abdicate in 1912. Sun Yat-sen, the leader of the newly formed Nationalist Party, declared China a republic and became the president.

▲ A group of Chinese men smoke in a 19th-century opium "den." When the Communists came to power in 1949 they led an antidrug campaign that stopped people from using opium.

◀ Puyi became China's last emperor at age three. He lost his throne three years later. In the 1930s the Japanese made him the emperor of their state in Manchuria, but he had no real power.

Civil War

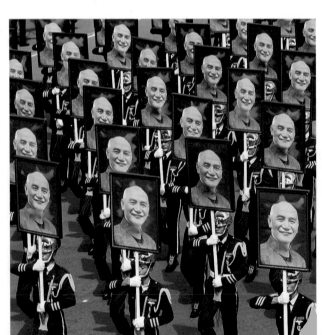

▲ Japanese troops ride into Manchuria. The invaders wanted access to the region's minerals.

▼ Taiwanese soldiers hold up posters of Chiang Kai-shek on Taiwan's National Day.

The Chinese disagreed about the best way forward. During the 1920s the Nationalists, now led by Chiang Kai-shek, fought rival warlords for control. They also had to fight a new enemy. Communists founded the Chinese Communist Party in 1921. They were inspired by the communist revolution that had taken place in Russia in 1917.

During the 1930s, Japan tried to increase its territory in China. Japanese troops took over Manchuria in 1931 and in 1937 fought their way to Nanjing, which was then the capital. The Nationalists and Communists both fought the Japanese, but when Japan was defeated in 1945, they again turned against one another.

After a bitter civil war, the Communists were victorious. In 1949, Mao Zedong proclaimed the People's Republic of China. Chiang led the Nationalists to Taiwan, where they set up the rival Republic of China.

Under Mao, all land belonged to the state. People worked on farms or in factories run by the government. The Soviet Union helped China develop its industries. People had little freedom, however, and could not question government decisions. Mao set tough targets for the production of food, and when harvests failed, many people starved to death.

CHAIRMAN MAO

Mao Zedong was born into a farming family. He became a Communist while working briefly as a librarian at the University of Peking. In the 1920s Mao helped the Communists win support among ordinary Chinese people. By the 1930s, he had become a leader in the Communist army fighting the Nationalists.

By 1934 the Nationalists had gained the upper hand. They surrounded the Communists in their stronghold. Mao made a smart decision. He led 100,000 of his followers on a grueling 6,000-mile (9,600-km) trek to the district of Yan'an. Many thousands died on what became known as the Long March, but the Communist Party survived. When the Communists won the civil war, Mao was chairman of the party. He began the enormous task of transforming China into a communist country.

▲ A massive portrait of Mao Zedong dominates Tiananmen Square in Beijing (Peking).

China's Varied Culture

AT CHINESE NEW YEAR, excited families line the streets of China's cities. Brightly colored giant figures of dragons twist and bob through the crowds as dancers work the models. The Chinese believe that the dragon dance brings good luck. When they get home, they eat special New Year foods for luck through the coming year. At midnight, loud firecrackers welcome the New Year. During the 1960s and 1970s the Chinese authorities frowned on scenes like this; they wanted to abandon China's old customs and traditions. Recently, though, government attitudes have relaxed. The Chinese have begun to celebrate their rich heritage. The dragon dance is again performed all over China—as well as in Chinese communities around the world.

◀ The Chinese see dragons as a sign of good fortune. In ancient times, dragon gods were believed to provide the rain and to protect travelers.

CHINA'S SHIFTING POPULATION

With a population of 1.3 billion, China has more people than any other country. About a third of the population lives in cities, with two-thirds in the country. However, these proportions are changing, as about 4 million country-dwellers move to cities each year, seeking work and a better life.

Many areas have too many farmers and not enough good land. Cities provide better-paid jobs and better schools and hospitals.

About 91 percent of China's population are Han Chinese. There are also 55 other ethnic groups, including Zhuang from the south, Hui from the north, Uygurs from the northwest, Tibetans, Tatars, and Mongols. Many of these groups have their own language and customs.

1952 / 575 million	1985 / 1,059 million
13% Urban / 87% Rural	24% Urban / 76% Rural

1995 / 1,211 million	2005 / 1,306 million
29% Urban / 71% Rural	43% Urban / 57% Rural

Common Chinese Phrases

Here are a few common phrases in Putonghua, or Mandarin, but you'll need to master the four tones of voice used in China to pronounce them properly!

First tone   [1]   High and level
Second tone   [2]   Starting low and rising
Third tone   [3]   Starting low, falling, then rising
Fourth tone   [4]   Starting high and falling

Phrases:

Hello / how are you?	Ni [2] hao [3] (nee how)
Goodbye	Zai [4] jia [4] (dzai-jyan)
Thank you	Xie [4] xie [4] (shyeh shyeh)
My name is...	Wo [3] jiao [4] (waw jyaow)

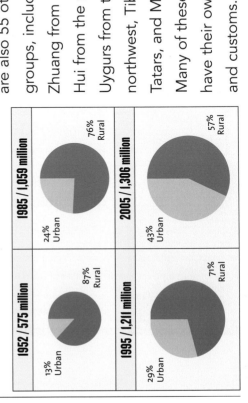

▲ Mongol children learn to ride early in life so they are not a burden when their family moves camp.

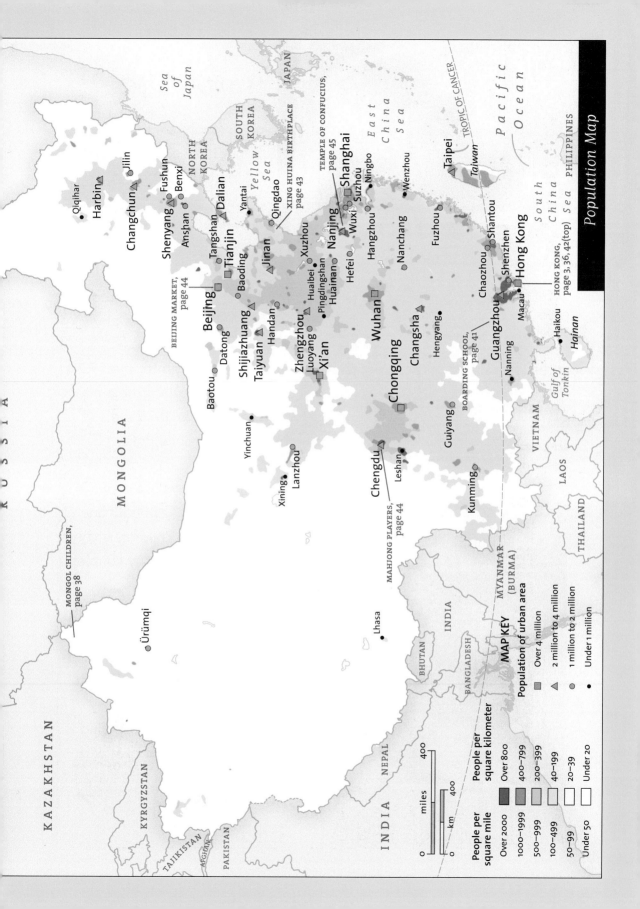

Population Map

MAP KEY

Population of urban area
- ■ Over 4 million
- ▲ 2 million to 4 million
- ● 1 million to 2 million
- • Under 1 million

People per square mile / **People per square kilometer**
- Over 2000 / Over 800
- 1000–1999 / 400–799
- 500–999 / 200–399
- 100–499 / 40–199
- 50–99 / 20–39
- Under 50 / Under 20

miles 0 ... 400
km 0 ... 400

MONGOL CHILDREN, page 38

BEIJING MARKET, page 44

XING HUINA BIRTHPLACE, page 43

TEMPLE OF CONFUCIUS, page 45

MAHJONG PLAYERS, page 44

BOARDING SCHOOL, page 41

HONG KONG, page 3, 36, 42(top)

KAZAKHSTAN
KYRGYZSTAN
TAJIKISTAN
AFGHAN.
PAKISTAN
INDIA
NEPAL
BHUTAN
BANGLADESH
MYANMAR (BURMA)
LAOS
THAILAND
VIETNAM
PHILIPPINES

RUSSIA
MONGOLIA

Ürümqi
Lhasa
Xining
Lanzhou
Yinchuan
Baotou
Datong
Taiyuan
Handan
Shijiazhuang
Xi'an
Luoyang
Zhengzhou
Chengdu
Leshan
Chongqing
Guiyang
Kunming
Nanning
Changsha
Hengyang
Wuhan
Nanchang
Hefei
Huainan
Pingdingshan
Huaibei
Xuzhou
Jinan
Qingdao
Yantai
Baoding
Tianjin
Beijing
Tangshan
Dalian
Anshan
Benxi
Fushun
Shenyang
Changchun
Jilin
Harbin
Qiqihar
Nanjing
Wuxi
Suzhou
Shanghai
Hangzhou
Ningbo
Wenzhou
Fuzhou
Chaozhou
Shantou
Shenzhen
Macau
Hong Kong
Guangzhou
Haikou
Hainan
Taipei
Taiwan

Sea of Japan
JAPAN
NORTH KOREA
SOUTH KOREA
Yellow Sea
East China Sea
South China Sea
Pacific Ocean
Gulf of Tonkin
TROPIC OF CANCER

为四化一对夫妇只生一个孩

Family Life

The family is a priority for the Chinese. Grandparents, parents, and children often share a home, although Chinese families are smaller than they used to be. Younger people often look after older family members. Respect for older people is one of the principles of the Chinese philosophy called Confucianism.

▲ Posters remind couples to limit their family to one child.

China's population grew so quickly after the 1950s that it threatened to become too large for the amount of food the country could produce. In 1979 the Communist Party created the One-Child Policy. Couples had to pay a fine if they had more than one child. The policy has been relaxed, but most families in China still have only one child, because bringing up children is very expensive. In country areas, many couples preferred their child to be a son, so he could help on the farm and support them in their old age. Baby girls were often abandoned, or even killed, so that couples could try again for a son. This means that males now outnumber females in many parts of China. Sons are often so spoiled by their parents that they are known as "little emperors."

▼ Junior high school students have to fit in a lot of studies: several sciences, history, English, and geography, as well as physical education.

Learning to Read and Write

Chinese children have to work hard at school. Everyone is supposed to have nine years of schooling, although children from poor families often quit school early to start work. School hours are long, lasting from 7:45 a.m. to 4 p.m. There used to be about 60 students in a class, but today the number is closer to 30. Learning to read and write is more of a challenge in China than in most-countries. The Chinese script is not based on letters that represent sounds, but on

▼ Young children take an afternoon nap after lunch at their boarding school.

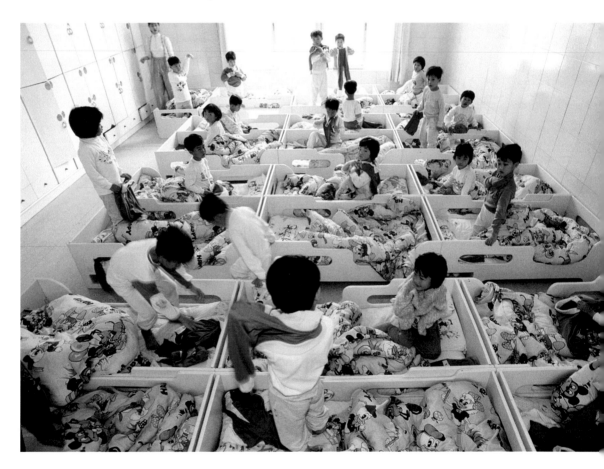

symbols called characters. There are between 50,000 and 60,000 characters in all. Children know about 6,000 by the time they go to high school.

The Arts

Arts and crafts have a long history in China. Thousands of years ago the Chinese were some of the first people to use materials such as silk, jade, bronze, wood, and paper to make works of art. Painters used brushes

▲ For many centuries the Chinese have used combinations of herbs and other plants to cure diseases. Today, Chinese medicine is popular in other countries—while the Chinese have begun to practice more Western medicine.

PORCELAIN

Chinese pottery is among the finest in the world. The earliest Chinese pottery dates back to 2000 B.C. Around A.D. 1300 potters discovered a valuable secret. They mixed fine clay with powdered rock and baked their creations at a high temperature. This produced a thin but strong type of pottery, which in Europe became known simply as "china." The finest blue-and-white porcelain dates from the Ming dynasty (right).

called calligraphy. Each character was drawn with smooth strokes of a brush. Government officials had to be skilled at calligraphy, painting, and writing poetry.

Sports and Pastimes

In the 1990s the Communist government brought in two-day weekends, and now most people work only five days a week. The government also added three weeklong holidays to the traditional one-day holidays on Chinese New Year, Labor Day, and National Day. The Chinese call the new holidays "golden weeks."

The Chinese love to play sports. The most popular include table tennis, volleyball, basketball, badminton, and soccer. Chinese athletes often win medals in major championships, and China was happy to be awarded the 2008 Olympics.

China's martial arts, or fighting arts, date back 3,000 years. There are hundreds of different styles, including kung fu, with their own techniques

NATIONAL HOLIDAYS

The Chinese year includes many festivals and holidays, some of which are just as important as the official holidays listed below.

JANUARY 1
New Year's Day

CHINESE NEW YEAR (also called Spring Festival) Takes place in January or February, depending on the lunar calendar

MARCH 8
International Women's Day

APRIL 1
Tree-planting Day

MAY 1
International Labor Day

MAY 4
Youth Day

JUNE 1
Children's Day

JULY 1
Communist Party Birthday

AUGUST 1
Army Day

OCTOBER 1
National Day

▼ Xing Huina does a victory lap after winning the 10,000-meter race at the 2004 Olympic Games.

43

▲ Mahjong is one of China's most popular games. Many players gamble on the outcome— it can be very expensive if they lose.

and ideas. People practice tai chi in parks all over China. This slow series of smooth movements began as a martial art. It is good exercise for the body and helps the mind relax.

Many Chinese homes are small, so people often relax outside. They fly kites in parks and play pool or table tennis on street tables or in clubs. There are also outdoor film shows, concerts, and even discos. Old men meet at teahouses over games of cards, chess, or mahjong.

Eating in China

Chinese cooking is enjoyed all over the world, but there is no single style. Food and ways of cooking vary in different areas. Rice is an important part of meals in the south, while dumplings and noodles are eaten in the north. Beijing duck and Mongolian hot pot are popular northern dishes. Sichuan cooking from western China is spicy, while Cantonese cuisine

▼ Most Chinese don't go to supermarkets. They buy their groceries from market stalls.

from the southeast is renowned for such quick cooking that the food is almost raw. Chinese people often eat plenty of fresh fruit and vegetables but little dairy produce, which makes for a healthy diet. They eat with chopsticks rather than with knives and forks.

Religion and Beliefs

China has no official religion, and most Chinese are not religious. Among those who follow a religion, Buddhism is the most popular faith. It arrived in China from India nearly 2,000 years ago. Confucianism and Taoism are two homegrown philosophies that are even older. There are also numbers of Muslims, Christians, and Jews.

CONFUCIUS

The Chinese philosopher Kongfuzi is known in the West as Confucius. A government official, he lived from 551 to 479 B.C. Confucius believed that life should be based on morality, kindness, and education. He also stressed the importance of seniority: The old educate the young, and the young respect the old. Confucius gained many followers, who recorded his sayings in a book called the *Analects.* During the Han dynasty, this book formed the basis of laws throughout China.

▶ Gold dragons flank a bronze statue of Confucius.

Modern China

RESIDENTS OF SHANGHAI still practice tai chi exercises on the banks of the Yangtze (Chang Jiang) River, as their ancestors have done for centuries. All around, however, their city is changing. In the last 20 years, it has grown so quickly that former residents hardly recognize it. On the skyline, cranes mark the construction sites for some of the tallest buildings in the world. On the streets, signs of economic success are everywhere, from new cars to shopping malls and cell phones.

Shanghai is an example of the dramatic changes that have swept much of China since the 1980s. The country has changed from a state that was mostly closed to outsiders to a thriving economy that wants to trade with the world.

◀ **Old and new: the skyscrapers of Shanghai provide a backdrop for early morning tai chi exercises on the bank of the Yangtze River.**

At a Glance

PUZZLE PIECES

China is divided into 23 provinces, five autonomous regions, four autonomous municipalities, and two Special Administrative Regions (SARs). The autonomous municipalities are four major cities: Beijing (Peking), Shanghai, Tianjin, and Chongqing. Hong Kong and Macau, the two SARs, are self-governing except in defense and foreign policy. Hong Kong, a British colony from the 1840s, was returned to China in 1997. It will remain mostly separate, with its own government and currency, until 2047 or later. Macau, a Portuguese colony from 1887 to 1999, has a similar position.

▼ In 1950 China invaded Tibet. Nine years later the Tibetan Spiritual Leader, the Dalai Lama, left the country. He remains an important figure for many Tibetans like this woman.

Trading Partners

Between the 1950s and 1980s, China's main trading partners were the Soviet Union, the Communist countries of Eastern Europe, and the countries of Asia. In recent years China has built up strong trading links with other nations. In 2001 China joined the World Trade Organization, which promotes free trade among its many members. China's chief exports include textiles and clothing, machinery, food, chemicals, and electronic products.

Country	Percent China exports
United States	21.4%
Hong Kong	16.3%
Japan	11.0%
South Korea	4.6%
All others combined	46.7%

Country	Percent China imports
Japan	15.2%
Taiwan	11.6%
South Korea	11.2%
United States	7.4%
All others combined	54.6%

Political Map

RUSSIA

KAZAKHSTAN

KYRGYZSTAN

TAJIKISTAN

PAKISTAN

MONGOLIA

HEILONGJIANG

Harbin

Changchun

JILIN

Shenyang

LIAONING

NORTH KOREA

SOUTH KOREA

Sea of Japan

JAPAN

NEI MONGOL (INNER MONGOLIA) AUTONOMOUS REGION

Ürümqi

XINJIANG UYGUR AUTONOMOUS REGION

Boundary claimed by India

AKSAI CHIN

Boundary claimed by China

Hohhot

JIUQUAN SATELLITE LAUNCH CENTRE page 56

COTTON FARMING page 55

Yinchuan

NINGXIA HUIZU AUTONOMOUS REGION

Xining

GANSU

Lanzhou

QINGHAI

XIZANG (TIBET) AUTONOMOUS REGION

Lhasa

NEPAL

BHUTAN

BANGLADESH

INDIA

Boundary claimed by China

MYANMAR (BURMA)

WOMAN AND CHILD page 48

SICHUAN

Chengdu

DENG XIAOPING BIRTHPLACE, page 52

Kunming

YUNNAN

LAOS

THAILAND

VIETNAM

TROPIC OF CANCER

BEIJING

Beijing (Peking)

HEBEI

TIANJIN

Tianjin

Shijiazhuang

SHANDONG

Jinan

Taiyuan

SHANXI

Zhengzhou

HENAN

Xi'an

SHAANXI

Wuhan

HUBEI

CHONGQING

Chongqing

Changsha

HUNAN

Guiyang

GUIZHOU

GUANGXI ZHUANGZU AUTONOMOUS REGION

Nanning

Gulf of Tonkin

HAINAN

Haikou

Macau

MACAU SPECIAL ADMINISTRATIVE REGION

GUANGDONG

Guangzhou (Canton)

Hong Kong

HONG KONG SPECIAL ADMINISTRATIVE REGION

SHENZHEN SPECIAL ECONOMIC ZONE, page 53, 55

JIANGXI

Nanchang

FUJIAN

Fuzhou

ZHEJIANG

Hangzhou

ANHUI

Hefei

JIANGSU

Nanjing

SHANGHAI

Shanghai

SHANGHAI, page 3, 46–47

Yellow Sea

OLYMPIC CELEBRATIONS, page 56 AND FORBIDDEN CITY page 57

East China Sea

DOUBLE TEN DAY CELEBRATIONS, page 51

Taipei

TAIWAN

The People's Republic of China claims Taiwan as its 23rd province. Taiwan's government (Republic of China) maintains that there are two political entities.

Taiwan Strait

South China Sea

PHILIPPINES

110°E

100°E

90°E

30°N

20°N

40°N

30°N

20°N

40°N

MAP KEY

⊛ National capital

⊙ Provincial capital

miles 0 — 400

km 0 — 400

HOW THE GOVERNMENT WORKS

China is an authoritarian state—a country ruled by a very powerful, centralized government. Although there are other parties, the Chinese Communist Party (CCP) dominates the government. Most senior officials are appointed, not elected, and almost all people in top jobs are CCP members. The General Secretary is also the President. The judges of the Supreme People's Court are appointed by the National People's Congress.

CHINESE COMMUNIST PARTY	GOVERNMENT	JUDICIARY	
GENERAL SECRETARY	PRESIDENT	SUPREME PEOPLE'S COURT COMMITTEE	
STANDING COMMITTEE	STATE COUNCIL—ABOUT 60 MEMBERS	SUPREME PEOPLE'S COURT	
POLITBURO			
CENTRAL COMMITTEE	NATIONAL PEOPLE'S CONGRESS— ABOUT 3,000 MEMBERS	LOCAL PEOPLE'S COURTS	SPECIAL PEOPLE'S COURTS
NATIONAL PARTY CONGRESS			

Minority Groups

▼ The "little red book" of quotations by Mao Zedong—also spelled Mao Tse-tung—has sold millions of copies.

Most Chinese are from the Han ethnic group, but China's five autonomous regions—Nei Mongol (Inner Mongolia), Guangxi, Ningxia (ning-she-ah), Xizang (Tibet), and Xinjiang (shin-jee-ong)—are home to large minority groups such as Uygurs and Tibetans. These regions have some rights to govern themselves, but they are still controlled by the central government. Relations between minority groups and the government have not been always happy. In 1950 Tibet lost its independent rule. Its spiritual leader, the Dalai Lama, fled to India. Many Tibetans hope for independence.

Cultural Revolution

In 1966 Mao Zedong launched a ten-year campaign against people who questioned the communist system. He called on young Chinese, particularly students, to stamp out the "Four Olds" in society: old customs, old traditions, old beliefs, and China's ancient culture.

Called Red Guards and taking their ideas from Mao's thoughts in his "little red book," young people began to seek out enemies of the government. They abandoned the tradition of showing respect to their elders and accused teachers, scholars, and even members of their own families of "mistaken ideas." Schools were closed. Millions of people were forced into manual work. Some were tortured or killed.

The Cultural Revolution was a disaster for China. A generation of children had no education. Factories and farms fell behind on production. The Communist Party lost many of its own leaders.

TAIWAN

The island of Taiwan became part of China in the 17th century, when Chinese settlers drove out many of the original inhabitants. At the end of China's civil war in 1949, the defeated Nationalists fled to the island and set up a government under the name of Republic of China (ROC). A few nations, such as the United States, recognized the ROC as the rightful government of all of China, even though the tiny island had no real power. During the 1970s, however, most nations recognized the Communists on the mainland as China's government. Taiwan meanwhile overtook its giant neighbor economically. It became wealthy through trade. Today, many people in Taiwan are determined to stay independent, but China sees Taiwan as a rebellious province.

▲ Taiwanese children celebrate Double Ten Day, the country's national day.

China Opens for Business

When Mao died in 1976, a time of sudden and dramatic change began in China. The new leader, Deng Xiaoping (dung shyaow peeng), was a reformer. He told the Chinese "to get rich is glorious"—the kind of statement that Mao would never have made. In just a few years, China modernized quickly. Deng was eager to deal with and learn from the West, as he signaled in the so-called Open Door Policy.

Deng loosened controls on farms. He began to sell off state-run businesses to private companies. The Chinese government set up four Special Economic Zones (SEZs) in Shenzhen, Zhuhai, Shantou, and Xiamen, where international companies could open factories and trade. They were later joined by Hainan Island. To attract foreign companies, the government offered special tax breaks and cheap land. It also relaxed trade rules, to make it easier for companies to operate. Fourteen larger cities were also opened to world trade, but with higher taxes.

A REFORMER

Deng Xiaoping was born in 1904. At age 16 he went to study in Paris, France, where he joined the communist movement. He was a close adviser of Mao Zedong during the civil war and became vice premier in 1952. He and Mao disagreed about the economy and Deng fell out of favor. After Mao's death, Deng finally moved back into a position of power. He became China's chief policymaker, bringing in a wide range of economic and social reforms.

The Tiananmen Square Massacre

Many Chinese hoped that the economic reforms of the 1980s would be matched by political change. In 1989 thousands of students and other citizens gathered in Tiananmen Square in Beijing (Peking) to protest corruption in the government and call for democracy. After six weeks, the government sent in the army to disperse the protesters. Exact numbers are not known, but troops likely killed more than 1,000 unarmed protesters and arrested 4,600.

China's record on human rights remains poor. It is still very difficult for people to organize a strike, campaign for better working conditions, or criticize government policy without running the risk of going to jail.

▲ Trucks wait in line at a customs post on their way to pick up cargo from Shenzhen, one of China's special economic zones.

China's Economy

Despite their political troubles, the Chinese have been rapidly developing their economic sector. The People's Republic of China is the world's fastest-growing economy. Since the 1980s the economy has expanded by a massive 9 or 10 percent each year, which is about

INDUSTRY & MINING

The map shows China's main centers for industry, mining, and manufacturing. These three elements make up 53 percent of the country's economy. Industry is still far more developed in southern and eastern China than in the north and west.

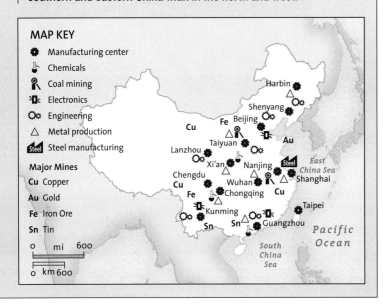

MAP KEY

- ⚙ Manufacturing center
- ⚗ Chemicals
- ⛏ Coal mining
- ⚡ Electronics
- ⚙ Engineering
- △ Metal production
- Steel Steel manufacturing

Major Mines

- **Cu** Copper
- **Au** Gold
- **Fe** Iron Ore
- **Sn** Tin

0   mi   600

0   km 600

Harbin

Shenyang

Beijing

Taiyuan

Lanzhou

Cu   Fe

Xi'an

Chengdu

Cu

Fe

Kunming

Sn

Nanjing

Wuhan

Chongqing   Cu

Sn

Guangzhou

Taipei

Au

Shanghai

East China Sea

Pacific Ocean

South China Sea

▼ **China produces two-thirds of all the toys in the world.**

four times quicker than Western economies. The keys to China's economic success are its huge workforce and plentiful natural resources, including iron ore, coal, and oil.

Agriculture was once the heart of the economy. It now earns only 12 percent of China's income, but nearly half of the population still works in farming. Industry and manufacturing are thriving. China's factories turn out half of the world's cameras and a third of its air conditioners and televisions.

Whether they work in agriculture or in industry, most Chinese earn far less than workers in developed countries. More and more, however, earn enough spare money to enjoy going shopping. In the last ten years, ownership of color TVs has increased by almost half. Cell phones are also very popular. The number of households with cell phones jumped from 10 percent in 1999 to 48 percent in 2004.

Protecting the Environment

Even in a country with as much space as China, industrial progress sometimes damages the natural world. The Chinese government is taking steps to protect the air from automobile exhaust and factory fumes, and the land and rivers from chemicals used in farming. One of its measures was to create a national tree-planting day. In the last five years almost 3 billion people have participated, planting 12 billion trees.

Another very exciting plan is to build a new ecocity called Dongtan, near Shanghai. Electricity will come from wind and wave power, and water will be collected from rainfall.

▲ China's family farms are small—but 46 million of them grow cotton, making China the world's leading cotton producer.

▼ China now manufactures many of the world's electronic goods.

▲ Crowds celebrate the news that China will host the 2008 Olympic Games.

▼ Yang Liwei, China's first astronaut, heads for his historic launch into outer space.

Looking to the Future

The 21st century opened with great hope. In 2001 China was awarded the 2008 Olympic Games in Beijing, beating out Canada, France, Turkey, and Japan. The Chinese scheduled the opening ceremony for 8 p.m. on August 8, 2008 (08-08-08-08). It will be a very lucky time and date, because in China the number 8 is associated with prosperity.

In 2003 China launched a crew into space, something only the United States and Russia had done before. To many people, the mission signaled China's arrival as a world superpower.

The remarkable changes of the last 20 years have posed many problems for the Chinese. The lives of rich and poor, for example, are now completely different. For some people in the country, life is as hard as it was for their ancestors centuries ago. Many families in the cities, on the other hand, are better off than ever. They want to use their money to live more comfortable lives.

One of the things the Chinese spend their money on is travel, both within China and to other countries. China's airports will be kept very busy, because the number of international tourists visiting China has also risen. By 2020, China will be the world's biggest tourist destination!

▼ The tiled roofs of Beijing's Forbidden City were once seen only by emperors and their officials, because everyone else was kept out of the area. Today, the City attracts millions of tourists.

Add a Little Extra to Your Country Report!

If you are assigned to write a report about China, you'll want to include basic information about the country, of course. The Fast Facts chart on page 8 will give you a good start. The rest of the book will give you the details you need to create a full and up-to-date paper or PowerPoint presentation. But what can you do to make your report more fun than anyone else's? If you use your imagination and dig a bit deeper into some of the topics introduced in this book, you're sure to come up with information that will make your report unique!

>Flag

Perhaps you could explain the history of China's flag and the meanings of its colors and symbols. Go to **www.crwflags.com/fotw/flags** for more information.

>National Anthem

How about downloading China's national anthem and playing it for your class? At **www.nationalanthems.info** you'll find what you need, including the words to the anthem in Chinese and English, plus sheet music for the anthem. Simply pick "C" and then "China" from the list on the left-hand side of the screen, and you're on your way.

>Time Difference

If you want to understand the time difference between China and where you are, this Web site can help: **www.worldtimeserver.com**. Just pick "China" from the list on the right. If you called China right now, would you wake whomever you are calling from their sleep?

>Currency

Another Web site will convert your money into yuan, the currency used in China. You'll want to know how much money to bring if you're ever lucky enough to travel to China: **www.xe.com/ucc**.

>Weather

Why not check the current weather in China? It's easy—simply go to **www.weather.com** to find out if it's sunny or cloudy, warm or cold in China right this minute! Pick "World" from the headings at the top of the page. Then search for China. Click on any city you like. Be sure to click on the tabs below the weather report for Sunrise/Sunset information, Weather Watch, and Business Travel Outlook, too. Scroll down the page for the 36-hour Forecast and a satellite weather map. Compare your weather to the weather in the Chinese city you chose. Is this a good season, weather-wise, for a person to travel to China?

>Miscellaneous

Still want more information? Simply go to National Geographic's One-Stop Research site at **www.nationalgeographic.com/onestop**. It will help you find maps, photos and art, articles and information, games and features that you can use to jazz up your report.

Glossary

Abdicate give up the throne and the power that goes with being a ruler.

Class social rank in society.

Communism a political and economic system in which property and the means of production, such as farms and factories, are owned by the state or by all the people; wealth is meant to be divided equally among all the inhabitants of the country or according to each person's need.

Delta a low-lying plain at the mouth of a river that is formed when soil and sand carried in the water settle on the riverbed near the river's exit to the sea. This sediment gradually builds up, partly blocking the river, which then splits into smaller branches before its waters empty into the sea.

Desert an extremely dry area, where yearly precipitation is usually less than 10 inches (250 mm).

Dynasty a series of rulers from the same family.

Ecocity a settlement with buildings that make the best possible use of natural sources such as sun, wind, and rain to supply the energy and water needs of the inhabitants, and where waste matter is reused or recycled.

Ecosystem a community of living things and the environment they interact with; an ecosystem includes plants, animals, soil, water, and air.

Habitat the environment where an animal or plant lives.

Lock an enclosure on a canal or a river with gates at each end. By opening and closing the gates, the water level can be varied to raise or lower boats.

Migration the repeated, usually seasonal, travels of animals (including humans) from one place to another in search of food, better weather, and better conditions in which to raise young.

Monsoon wind a seasonal wind. During the winter, a cool northeast wind blows across China bringing dry, pleasant weather; in the summer, a southwest wind brings heavy downpours of rain.

Philosophy a search for truth or wisdom through reasoning; also the general beliefs of an individual or group.

Plateau a large, relatively flat area that rises high above the surrounding land.

Pollution the release of harmful substances into the air, water, or soil.

Porcelain a fine, strong, white material made by baking a mixture of kaolin (china clay) and petuntze (china stone) at a very high temperature.

Rain forest an area of dense, broad-leafed evergreen trees and vines with little undergrowth, receiving at least 80 inches (200 cm) of rainfall per year on average.

Species a type of organism; animals or plants in the same species look similar and can only breed successfully among themselves.

Subarctic a region just outside the Arctic Circle, which is an imaginary line drawn around the Earth parallel to the Equator and 66.5 degrees north of it.

Tropical a climate with sufficiently warm temperatures and rainfall to support plant growth throughout the year.

Bibliography

Charley, Catherine. *China* (Country Fact File Series). London: Simon & Schuster, 1994.

Goddard, C. *China*. London: Evans Brothers Ltd, 2004.

http://archaeology.about.com/od/china/index.htm
(history and archaeology links)

http://english.gov.cn/index.htm
(government Web site)

http://www.china.org.cn/english/index.htm
(general information)

Further Information

NATIONAL GEOGRAPHIC Articles

Busch, Richard. "Return of the People's Republic." NATIONAL GEOGRAPHIC TRAVELER (March 1993): 32-38.

Edwards, Mike. "Han Dynasty." NATIONAL GEOGRAPHIC (February 2004): 2-29.

Ellis, William S. "Shanghai: Where China's Past and Future Meet." NATIONAL GEOGRAPHIC (March 1994): 2-35.

Hessler, Peter. "The New Story of China's Ancient Past." NATIONAL GEOGRAPHIC (July 2003): 56-81.

Jasper, Becker. "China's Growing Pains." NATIONAL GEOGRAPHIC (March 2004): 68-95.

Kohl, Larry. "Above China." NATIONAL GEOGRAPHIC (March 1989): 278-311.

Larmer, Brook. "The Manchurian Mandate." NATIONAL GEOGRAPHIC (September 2006): 42-73.

Lindesay, William. "The Great Wall." NATIONAL GEOGRAPHIC TRAVELER (October 1999): 234-235.

Terrill, Ross. "Hong Kong: Countdown to 1997." NATIONAL GEOGRAPHIC (February 1991): 100-131.

Wilkinson, Julia, and Lindesay, William. "Heart of the Celestial Empire." NATIONAL GEOGRAPHIC TRAVELER (September 1998): 84-102.

Web sites to explore

More fast facts about China, from the CIA (Central Intelligence Agency): www.cia.gov/cia/publications/factbook/geos/ch.html

The Chinese National Tourist Office welcomes you with all sorts of information about

China—past and present: www.cnto.org

Who are the Fuwa (the Friendlies)? Find out about the official mascots of the Beijing 2008 Olympic Games and more: http://en.beijing208.com/

Passionate about pandas? Check out National Geographic's "creature feature" on pandas, which includes links to other cool panda sites: www.nationalgeographic.com/kids/creature_feature/0011/pandas.html

Curious about the Three Gorges Dam? An Online News Hour from PBS discusses the project and presents an interview with a National Geographic author and photographer who covered the topic for NATIONAL GEOGRAPHIC magazine: www.pbs.org/newshour/bb/asia/july-dec97/gorges_10-8.html

Index

Credits

Picture Credits

Front Cover—Spine: Keren Su/Corbis; Top: Peter Adams/zefa/Corbis; Lo far left: Craig Lovell/Corbis; Lo left: Keren Su/Corbis; Lo right: Craig Lovell/Corbis; Lo far right: Jose Fuste Raga/Corbis

Interior—Corbis: 33 lo; Dave Bartruff: 50 lo; Bettmann: 52 lo; S. Carmona: 43 lo; China Features/Corbis Sygma: 56 up; Christie's Images: 26 up; Daniel J. Cox: 2 right, 16-17; Tim Davis: 23 lo; EPA: 14 lo; Hulton Deutsch Collection: 33 up, 34 up; Wolfgang Kaehler: 22 lo; Alain Le Gassmer: 40 up; Liu Liqun: 15 lo; Jose Fuste Raga: 2 left, 6-7; Roger Ressmeyer: 35 up; Keren Su: 45 lo; Dung Vo Trung: 55 lo; Julia Waterlow;Eye Ubiquitous: 13 up; Lee White 32 up; Xinhua/Xinhua Photo: 56 lo; Michael S.Yamashita: 44 up; NG Image Collection: Dr. M. Cynthia Beall and Dr. C. Melvyn Goldstein: 38 up; Jonathan Blair: 42 lo; Jodi Cobb: 34 lo, 51 lo; Stuart Franklin: 44 lo; Raymond Gehman: TP, 15 up, 57 lo; Melvyn Goldstein: 21 up; Justin Guariglia: 3 left, 3 right, 36-37, 40 lo, 46-47; Monika Klum: 11 up; O.Louis Mazzatenta: 2-3, 24-25, 29 lo; Mark W. Moffett: 10 lo, 23 up; Richard Nowitz: 5 up, 42 up, 59 up; Winfield Parks: 30 lo; Roy Toft: 21 lo; George Steinmetz: 12 lo, 55 up; Michael S.Yamashita: 29 up, 41 lo, 48 up, 53 up; Lu Zhi: 20 up; NPL: Mark Carwardine: 18 up; Shutterstock: Todd Taulman: 30 up; Steven Vona: 54 lo.

Map on pg.19: "WDPA Consortium 2006 World Database on Protected Areas web-download" - Copyright UNEP-World Conservation Monitoring Centre (UNEP-WCMC), 2006."

Text copyright © 2006 National Geographic Society
Published by the National Geographic Society.
All rights reserved. Reproduction of the whole or any part of the contents without written permission from the National Geographic Society is strictly prohibited. For information about special discounts for bulk purchases, contact National Geographic Special Sales: ngspecsales@ngs.org

For more information, please call 1-800-NGS-LINE (647-5463) or write to the following address:

NATIONAL GEOGRAPHIC SOCIETY
1145 17th Street N.W.
Washington, D.C. 20036-4688 U.S.A.

Visit the Society's Web site at www.nationalgeographic.com

Library of Congress Cataloging-in-Publication Data available on request
ISBN-10: 0-7922-6180-1
ISBN-13: 978-0-7922-6180-3

Printed in Belgium

Series design by Jim Hiscott.
The body text is set in Avenir; Knockout.
The display text is set in Matrix Script.

Front Cover—Top: Chinese grandfather holding baby; Lo far left: Chinese opera performer in Chengdu; Lo left: Silhouette on Yellow Mountains in Anhui Province; Lo right: Giant panda eating bamboo in Chengdu; Lo far right: Gate at Plaza in Kunming

Page 1—The moon over the Great Wall; Icon image on spine, Contents page, and throughout: A forest of bamboo in Hangzhou, China

Produced through the worldwide resources of the National Geographic Society

John M. Fahey, Jr., *President and Chief Executive Officer*; Gilbert M. Grosvenor, *Chairman of the Board*; Nina D. Hoffman, *Executive Vice President, President of Books Publishing Group*

National Geographic Staff for this Book

Nancy Laties Feresten, *Vice President, Editor-in-Chief of Children's Books*
Bea Jackson, *Director of Design and Illustration*
Virginia Koeth, *Project Editor*
David M.Seager, *Art Director*
Lori Epstein, *Illustrations Editor*
Stacy Gold, *Illustrations Research Editor*
Carl Mehler, *Director of Maps*
Priyanka Lamichhane, *Assistant Editor*
R. Gary Colbert, *Production Director*
Lewis R. Bassford, *Production Manager*
Vincent P. Ryan, Maryclare Tracy, *Manufacturing Managers*

Brown Reference Group plc. Staff for this Book

Project Editor: Sally MacEachern
Designer: Dave Allen
Picture Manager: Becky Cox
Maps: Martin Darlinson
Artwork: Darren Awuah
Index: Kay Ollerenshaw
Senior Managing Editor: Tim Cooke
Design Manager: Sarah Williams
Children's Publisher: Anne O'Daly
Editorial Director: Lindsey Lowe

About the Author

JEN GREEN received a doctorate from the University of Sussex, United Kingdom, in 1982. She worked in publishing for 15 years and is now a full-time writer who has written more than 150 books for children on natural history, geography, the environment, history, and other subjects.

About the Consultants

DR. GEORGE WEI is chair and associate professor of history at Susquehanna University. He is a specialist in Chinese and Asian history. Dr. Wei has lived and taught in China and has published extensively in both English and Chinese. He has led many study groups to China in recent years.

DR. HANCHAO LU is a professor of history and director of graduate studies at the School of History, Technology, and Society at the Georgia Institute of Technology. He is a specialist in industrialization and urbanization in China. His many publications include the prize-winning book *Beyond the Neon Lights: Everyday Shanghai in the Early Twentieth Century* (1999) and *Street Criers: A Cultural History of Chinese Beggars* (2005). Dr. Lu travels frequently to China for research.

Time Line of
Chinese History

BC **ca 1700** The Shang dynasty takes control of the Yellow (Huang) River delta.

551 Birth of Confucius.

221 The Qin ruler Shi Huangdi unites all of northern China and becomes its first emperor. Under his rule, the defensive wall along China's border is strengthened and extended, becoming what we know today as the Great Wall of China.

150 Buddhism is introduced to China.

AD **1000** The Chinese begin to use gunpowder in war.

1209 Genghis Khan unites Mongols and begins invasion of northern China.

1252 Kublai Khan (the grandson of Genghis Khan) invades China.

1271 Venetian explorer Marco Polo travels the entire Silk Road, an important trading route from Constantinople (Istanbul) to Chang'an (Xi'an) that connects China with Europe. The route branches north to Khanbalik (Beijing) and south to Shanghai.

1368 The Mongols are driven out of China by rebel forces and the Ming dynasty comes to power.

1417 Construction of the Forbidden City (in modern-day Beijing) begins. Today, this is the largest complex of ancient buildings in the world.

1689 Treaty of Nerchinsk signed with Russia; China's first official treaty with a European country.

1839 The Chinese government takes drastic measures to suppress the opium trade, seizing thousands of chests of illegal opium, many of them British. The British retaliate, and the First Opium War begins.

1842 Britain decisively overpowers China, and the war ends with the Treaty of Nanjing, under which China cedes the island of Hong Kong to Britain, and grants them extensive trading rights within the rest of the country.

1894 War breaks out between China and Japan, over control of Korea. China is defeated, and compelled to recognize Korea's independence, as well as allow Japan more trading rights. This adds to Chinese resentment of Japan.

1900 A coalition of antiforeign and anti-Christian groups rises up in what is known as the Boxer Rebellion. They attack missionary stations, Chinese Christians, and foreign posts. This provokes a retaliation by those foreign powers, at the end of which China is forced to yield even more privileges to foreigners in their country.

1911 With the Republican Revolution, the last Chinese emperor is forced to abdicate in 1912 and the Republic of China is established, under the newly formed Nationalist Party.

1914 World War I breaks out in Europe; Japan joins the Allies against Germany and seizes the German province of Shadong in China.

1917 China enters the war against Germany, partially in hopes of regaining the Shadong province.